The Storyteller & The Writer: Part I - The Writer

Cassie Fritsche

BookLeaf Publishing

Presentation by *BookLeaf Publishing*

Web: www.bookleafpub.com

E-mail: info@bookleafpub.com

ISBN: 9789358736182

First edition 2023

*To My Story Teller and husband, Scott. We
saved each other. Now, let me count the ways
that I love you...*

The Storyteller & The Writer

It wasn't supposed to happen
Magic shouldn't be real
He stays up all night,
Telling her his stories
His battles fought, abroad and at home
He tells her she's special
She warned him not to fall in love with her
She writes for him and bares her soul
She sees through the stories into his lonely heart
Both are weary from neglect and abuse
And then it happened
A light across the water, a firefly in the night
They are drawn to each other
She asks him to never stop telling his stories
He reads every word she writes and begs for
more
Their souls' milk and honey mingle
Sweet perfection to the lips
The storyteller fell in love with the writer
And the writer fell in love with her storyteller
and herself too
Words spoken or written will never do their
story justice
Their love an eternal magic, written in history

Purple

I've never believed in soulmates
I knew only oxytocin and dopamine
But your words are electricity running through
my veins,
Burning a path to my soul
You've captured my spirit and returned it with a
bit of your own
Your blue to my red
Now purple and messy and wonderful
A smile that could light up a forest
And quell a lonely heart
My pulse is rhythmic and synchronized to the
sound of your voice
So many feelings I can't comprehend
Or attribute to chemical reactions
Something magic. Something dark
Something stirred in the depths of my heart
Paint me with our purple
And light me with your fire again and again

Brick & Mortar

When the burdens of life feel too heavy
The conflict, the grief, the loneliness
Weighing my heart down to its depths
You build me up
You comfort me and encourage me until I'm me
again
Unique in our relationship,
You fill my every crack where my emptiness
shows
Understanding my complex mind and fearful
heart
We are what we need each other to be
Molding our compassion to fix the other
Yet we love all the imperfections
In another life, we'd be together
In another life this safe place would be home
But we've let our walls down, a rare occurrence
And we've granted access for one
You fix me
You love me
You are me, a reflection of my soul
And in our brick space, we are one

Worry Stone

I carry you with me
Like a worry stone in my pocket
Each time life is chaos
Or my burdens are too heavy
I rub the stone and focus
I know every facet, every flaw
What seems an ordinary rock,
Discarded and neglected
Has become my lifeline
But like the dark side of the moon
Always there in the shadows
My treasured stone is hidden
You are not the shiny diamond
That rests on my finger
Beautiful to the world around me
But sharp on my finger tips
You are worn and familiar
You are my comfort and rescuer
You are no longer neglected and cold
And I will carry you with me always

Beautiful Disaster

5

The walls should have been white and clean
Paint is for paper, my father warned
But my beautiful little girl wants to be an artist
She paints me flowers and horses on the walls
She paints in reds and blues,
Creating the beautiful purple she was formed
from
She leaves hand prints on doors and our hearts
The room is a multicolored mess
The pristine order turned chaos
She looks at me, so proud of herself
"Mommy, I painted for you"
The destruction is her masterpiece
I pick her up and with tears of pride,
I tell her "thank you, darling. It's beautiful"

Our Circus

My deepest hurt turned into a metaphor
Used against me like a weapon for years
Feeling like a burden, like chaos
You took that cruel image
And you showed me your magic
You transformed a weapon into flowers for me
I am not a circus of chaos, you said
I fly from the trapeze into the air
You hold onto me, but never weigh me down
I dive through air like a swan,
but you never let me hit the ground
You say our circus is a dance
Graceful and elegant in its rhythms
You embrace the highs and lows,
Matching my movements
You act as my safety net, never letting me fall
Our circus is beautiful and everlasting

Love and Other Drugs

Mania and Depression are clinical words
Cold and sterile and uncomfortable
Requiring so many pills and doctor's visits
My brain splayed open for review
Dysfunctional ion channels over here
Emotional trauma over there
I am a problem to be fixed
I have an illness needing a cure
This is how I've felt for years
A medical curiosity, a lab rat
Swallowing pills and going to therapy
A robotic ritual for self-repair
And then I found my drug of choice
Lifting my mood from 1 to 10, almost like
magic
The neurochemistry of oxytocin and dopamine
Is anything but magic, but you are
You light my veins on fire and an ache in my
chest
You fill my head with fantasies and my heart
with love
Love is most assuredly a drug, my dear
Changing my body and brain with each day
I am addicted to this cure
Lifting my depression and anchoring my mania

Restoring homeostasis to my life
I still take my pills and go to therapy
But I know that you are what makes me better
You are what makes me "me" again

Anticipation

Your plane will arrive soon
We'll share our first embrace
We've been so far apart
And now finally, in the same place

After months of baring our souls
Our vulnerabilities and grief
Our dreams for the future
Our happiness beyond belief

We know each other like our names
Each crack, each wall
We love deeper because of them
Not despite what others call flaws

We've been more ourselves
Than decades of our masks
Trying to please others
Hoping their attention would last

Shedding each layer of regret
Building each layer of respect and trust
Our love will last beyond our bodies
The purest kind, devoid of cheap lust

Your plane will arrive soon
I tremble with excitement
The rest of my life will start now
My smile and heart are vibrant

Unbalanced Equation

Broken flasks and burned lab books
The acrid smell of disappointment
If only this explosion were physical
We reacted, you and I, violently
Adding one drop of your docile nature
To 3 drops of my volatile one
Add in a dash of loneliness,
A pinch of neglect
And 2 heaping tablespoons of
People's perceived disapproval
BAM!
Our solution, our marriage, explodes
You said I was too reactive
That this was all my fault
Logically, I recount the ingredients
Was I not supportive enough?
Did I not sacrifice enough?
On my end of the equation,
What did I do wrong to cause this?
To experiment,
I swap out your side of the equation
For him
3 drops of my emotional mess
To 3 drops of his patience
A dash of hard learned lessons

A pinch of longing for affection
And 4 heaping tablespoons of
Love that overflows
Seamlessly, the solution blends
I was not the reactionary chemical
We were simply an unbalanced equation

The Child and the Monster

We've been disfigured by them
Emotionally beaten and bruised
Neglected and discarded
Until only shards of us remain
He is the child
Promising me a life he never intended to give
His constant need for approval
Fills the place a wife should take
His neglect suffocated me
She is the monster
Calculated and cunning
Spinning her webs of manipulations
Greed and gluttony snuff out
Any love there might have been for you
They are both reactionary and self-absorbed
The results are the same
Broken and ashamed,
Blaming ourselves for their crimes
1st degree murder of your marriage
Involuntary manslaughter of mine
Just the two of us at the crime scene
Making macabre jokes to pass time
Discussing murder weapons like gossip
She used money and children
He used neglect and emotional distance

We compare notes to find clues
Suddenly, it makes sense
We are victims, not criminals
The blood on our hands
Is our own, trying to stop the bleeding
Trying to save these marriages
For so long, as they just watched
As they stood by and criticized
"Don't let anyone see this mess!" He says
"You are not enough!" She screams
With bloody hands and hearts,
We clutch each other
Hoping the last bit of warmth from each other
Will save us
And it does

Bliss

Your favorite word is "Bliss"
You say it several times a day
Describing what we have with a 5 letter word
even though it should take thousands
I've been in a locked room
its walls covered in my desperate poetry
You asked me to unlock the door
I gave you puzzles and riddles to qualify you
I cautiously let you in
You studied my walls, taking in every detail
You took time to acknowledge my history, my
pain
Then, you took my hand and led me out
You showed me your heart and it was like a
mansion
Room after room of your history, your pain
I wept for you
As you unlocked each door for me, my love
grew
You displayed your soul for me
And then you handed me the keys
"What's mine is yours and what's yours is mine"
You've given me the keys to your mansion
You've given me little feet to run around it
We've built this life together

Our broken pieces fitting together as the
foundation
And now, finally, we are bliss

August

I wrote about him and our Julys
I wrote that July was our month, our bookends
What month comes after July?
August

You are my August
My new beginning, my fresh start
The crazy chaos with hurricanes and waning
summer sun
You are warm when you hold me
You cradle my head in your hands and kiss my
head

Once upon a time, August felt like it would
never come
And now, 2 Augusts in, it is my favorite time
A time for school supplies and autumn
decorations
A time for summer memories
And the kiss of the crisp air that is to come

You are my August
My warmth before the cold
I look forward to a lifetime of Augusts
And you'll be there, by my side

Colorblind

I spent 30 years seeing a monochromatic version
of the plain existence I thought was mine
I was relegated to my little house
"Our little slice of heaven"
I decorated my cage elegantly
I surrounded myself with pretty things and
plants
Convincing the little girl inside me that this was
happiness
You called me on my bullshit
Remember when I got so angry?
When you told me it wasn't ignorant bliss?
When you told me how neglected and
disrespected I was?
I was angry because I knew it was true
My black and white world was too restraining
But it's all I knew
And then there was you
There were suddenly reds and blues and purples
You took my breath away
Just by showing me color
Just by opening my eyes to more than my little
world
You ruined me in a way

How could I go back to seeing in black and
white,
when you were backlit by a rainbow?
You knew my soul
My love for adventure and nature's beauty
Now I see all the colors of a prism
Our world is a chaotic mess of colors
Like Alice falling into wonderland
My world is ever changing and completely
fascinating
And it's all because of you

Rescued

You rescued me from drowning
I lost my buoy and I didn't know which way
land was
You scooped me up and dried me off
Like it was nothing to you
But it was everything to me

I rescued you from the fire
It blazed around you, consuming everything
I ran in and reached for your hand
When you took it,
We ran together before the roof collapsed

We are rescuing them
We are showing our boys the way to the surface
how to breathe while being smothered
We are teaching them to rescue themselves
from all the horrors of that house

We are a family of rescuers now
Love will always be worth the risk

Ice cream vs. Water

He didn't always treat me badly
He treated me like I was an option
Like someone offered him an ice cream after a
big dinner
"Oh alright, sure, I'll make a little room"

You treat me like I'm water in the desert
Like I am the only option for you to survive
I'm the breath in your lungs
I'm the blood in your veins
I know you'll never treat me as if I'm just an
option
I'll always be a need instead of a want to you

More Than Riches

You say you don't deserve me
With zeroes on your bank account,
You feel no woman would accept you

But you have given me a treasure far more
precious than riches
You have given me a love that I have always
deserved,
but didn't think existed

You have given me children,
The family I have craved for so long
You have given me hope when I sat in darkness

You feel you have nothing to offer me, darling
But you have offered me our own version of
paradise
And I will always be grateful for you

Rewrote Our Stars

Our paths were set on others
Locked into vows we planned would last
Duty and loyalty came first
The hope of perfection, long past

When I met you, it felt like a cosmic rebirth
We realigned our lives to be one
I was the moon, dancing in the dark
And you were my dazzling sun

Rewriting the stars is never easy
We found that out the hard way
But nothing worth doing is ever easy
You make it more than worth it to stay

We gave ourselves a second chance
At happiness and a love worth sharing
We'll continue to dance through the night
Just like on the night we were married

Thank you, my darling, for showing me
Exactly what true love can be

Thank you for rewriting our stars
And giving me a wonderful life that is ours

Your Eyes

The most sparkling green I've ever seen
Brilliant like olive sapphires
More beautiful than rippling streams

When tears well up in your eyes,
I see my future
I see rocking chairs on a front porch
And children playing in the yard
I see adventures, big and small

Eyes are windows to the soul
And your eyes, my darling
reflect the purest soul I've encountered

Dance with me in our kitchen
So I can be mesmerized
By your glassy green eyes
Lighting up the night
And sparking a fire in my heart

My Favorite Dumbass

Until now, I've sung your triumphs and written
your praises
But no one is perfect, and that means you too
You are my favorite dumbass
In all the dumbass things you do

How are you my dumbass?
Let me count the ways
Marrying a spidery catfish on day one
And then continuing to stay

Let's not forget the lie you told
When I almost walked away
Or the time you went to prison
for that dumbass joke you made

You will always be my favorite dumbass
because I see your failures and your flaws
Knowing neither of us are perfect
I'll give my dumbass all of the applause

Loving Me Louder

You love me louder
You love me and I can hear it
I'm under water, light and sound muffled
It's dark and cold and devoid of feeling
But you love me louder
You love me with your words of encouragement
Giving me the strength to swim
You love me with your arms around me
Spreading your warmth before numbness takes
over
You love me in the morning and at night
And in the little moments between
You love me so I don't forget
You love where I am, under the oceans of my
mind
Not just on the shore, in the light
You love me louder, and louder still
When I cannot love myself, you remind me
Telling me about the girl who won your heart
And then you remind me again and again
So that I can love her too
You jumped into the cold water
Not forcing me to the surface
You understood
The comfort in being with me under my ocean
And you love me as loud as you can

www.ingramcontent.com/pod-product-compliance
Lightning Source LLC
Chambersburg PA
CBHW071245140726
47996CB00007B/2756